MW00988663

TO: _____

FROM: _____

THE
ENERGY
CLOCK

3 Simple Steps to
Create a Life Full of ENERGY—
and Live Your Best Every Day

MOLLY FLETCHER

Photo Credits
Internal images © page x, Maskot/Getty Images; page xii, Tim Robberts/Getty Images; page 4, Atit Phetmuangtong/EyeEm/Getty Images; page 14, Jetta Productions Inc/Getty Images; page 34, Westend61/Getty Images; page 50, M_a_y_a/Getty Images; page 56, d3sign/Getty Images; page 64, Ken Chernus/Getty Images; page 68, Kevin Kozicki/Getty Images; page 74, Klaus Vedfelt/Getty Images; page 80, Sarinya Pinngam/EyeEm/Getty Images; page 86, Astrakan Images/Getty Images; page 92, Thomas Barwick/Getty Images; page 96, Cavan Images/Getty Images; page 98, Hero Images/Getty Images; page 104, Hero Images/Getty Images; page 112, Deby Suchaeri/Getty Images
Internal images on pages vi, 8, 27, and 49 have been provided Unsplash; these images are licensed under CC0 Creative Commons and have been released by the author for public use.

Published by Simple Truths, an imprint of Sourcebooks
P.O. Box 4410, Naperville, Illinois 60567-4410
(630) 961-3900
sourcebooks.com

Printed and bound in China.
OGP 10 9 8 7 6 5

MY FAMILY—

thank you for the energy
you give others and me.

MY TEAM—

thank you for your belief in
our mission to help others
unleash their potential.

JIM LOEHR—

you taught me the power and
importance of managing our
energy. I cherish our friendship.

CONTENTS

INTRODUCTION

I REMEMBER ONE DAY IN MY LATE TWENTIES, STILL
early into my career as a sports agent, I was at lunch
with my parents. They had flown down from Michigan
to visit me in Atlanta and were only in town for a few
days. Just hours after they landed, we went straight to
a cool spot for lunch. We sat down, excited to connect,
and no one was more excited than me.

However, during lunch, my phone rang constantly
with clients calling—baseball players on their way to

the field, golfers leaving a practice round, coaches assessing their next game—and I took every call without hesitation. To say I wasn't really present was a *huge* understatement.

As I chatted with clients, the two people who are the most important people in the world to me ate a lunch they could have enjoyed a whole lot more back at home in Michigan. They sure didn't need to travel 775 miles to watch me on the phone!

Finally, my mom looked at me after a few calls and said, "What do they want?"

And I turned the fire-hose right on her:

One of my golfers needs new logoed apparel sent to the tournament this week.

One of my baseball players thinks he's getting traded.

My boss wants an update on one of my baseball prospects.

My coach's wife is calling me about a new head-coaching job that opened up.

One of my agents needs me in a meeting this afternoon regarding a pending deal.

My broadcaster wants to add more games to her schedule.

As I rattled them off, I could also see a more important message in my mom's eyes.

You just don't get it, Molly.

It was a moment that I never will forget. A moment I realized I wasn't being present with who mattered most. I had been afraid to not answer the calls, but as soon as I ended the last one, the truth hit.

If I hadn't taken those calls right at that moment, what would have happened? Would those clients have fired me? No way. I had filled their cups (or overflowed them) plenty.

I was acting just like one of those people quick to wear business as a badge of honor, but in that moment, my parents took me back down to earth. They didn't care about the high-profile athletes and coaches blowing up my phone. They just wanted to

know if I was taking care of myself, getting my rest, and enjoying my work and friends. This part of their love for me usually gave me such energy, but this time I had blocked all that good juju by answering my phone when I could have been present with them.

I got up from that lunch more exhausted than when I sat down—exhausted and conflicted, really. I felt bad they had flown all that way to listen to me talk on the phone for the first few hours of their visit.

I wished I had put my phone in my purse for forty-five minutes, and then fully engaged with my clients after lunch. It wasn't guilt. *It was failure to behave in a way that was consistent with my values.* Giving 50 percent never feels good, and people can tell when we are only half-present.

If we're lucky, we have people in our lives who help us set our energy clocks—who remind us what's truly important. My parents did that (and still do at times) for me, and every day I am mindful of doing the same for my three daughters.

But eventually, we have to set the energy clock for ourselves, and it is rooted in clarity around who and what matters most to us and putting our energy toward those things.

PART

1

AUDITING YOUR ENERGY

OUR TIME ON THIS EARTH IS LIMITED, BUT WHAT WE DO with our time and how we show up for moments in time is up to us. We can make our greatest impact not just by showing up but by showing up prepared and ready to engage. But that can only happen if we have enough energy for those moments.

The energy clock will help us be more intentional about who, what, and where we choose to invest our energy. We don't get to dictate the time we have on earth, but we *can* take charge of our energy.

We share our energy with our teams, our families, our employees, and our friends. The trick comes when we realize we need to give it exclusively to the things and the people that deserve it—that deserve you. In order to live intentionally, we need to be protective of our energy and constantly ensure who and what we give our energy to align with what matters most. When we do that, we make our greatest contributions to our colleagues, teams, family, and communities, and we find meaning for ourselves.

Have you ever noticed how most of us are obsessed with managing our time, with little thought to where we invest our energy?

We measure our years by months, our months by weeks, our weeks by days, our days by hours, and the hours by minutes. We fill our schedules to the max, and we measure our productivity by our level of activity.

This *quickly* becomes unsustainable. If unchecked, it's downright destructive.

If we don't bring energy to our time, does the time spent really matter anyway?

And if we misdirect our energy toward the wrong priorities, isn't it inevitable that we risk chasing the wrong things?

Here's the hard truth: If we don't decide what is most important to us, the world will decide for us.

Most of us live by the clock. We look at our watches, our phones, and our clocks all day, every day. Where do we need to be and when? How much time is this going to take? How can I move faster, get faster, live faster?

Google Maps tells us how long it will take for us to get to where we're going and how we can save two precious minutes by selecting the fastest route available. Most of us wake up to alarms and live our lives by notifications. We can't remember if Siri and Alexa are just apps or a legitimate part of our families.

Clocks remind us where we need to be *next*, not

where we are *right now*. They're a constant reminder that our time—which we've put on a pedestal—is slipping away or (worse yet) being wasted.

Our clocks beep, chirp, sing, and quack. They make us feel more panicked and rushed than present. It seems like we are always making the choice between "Not enough time" and "Why am I wasting my time?"

But we trudge on, because time is ticking and we have a schedule to keep. It is so bad that we even build in our breaks! "Oh perfect, I have enough time for five minutes for mindfulness and a bathroom break between these two meetings! Just what I need!"

Instead of shoving our needs between tasks, we need to think about what we *actually* need in order to feel fulfillment and accomplish work that is meaningful. The energy clock is not about managing our time—it is about reimagining our time. It's a challenge to reframe the passage of time as an investment of energy…an investment of energy into what matters most at work and at home. It challenges us to assess who and what deserves our energy and why.

Imagine checking your energy clock to ensure you are connected and present—rather than merely on time. Wouldn't that make all the difference? Imagine protecting your time by filling it with what matters most.

When we envision our energy clock, we ensure we are aligning what is meaningful to us with our energy outputs, and in doing so, we likely avoid waking up one day and realizing we are *way* off course. It's like a flight from New York to Los Angeles. We make slight

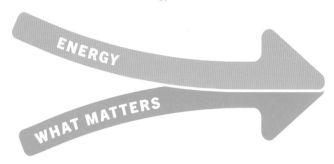

adjustments on the way due to wind and weather to arrive at our destination. Slight pivots keep us on course.

Life can be like that too. The path isn't always linear. Priorities change. Pivots need to be made. Learning to take ownership of our energy is the most important shift we can make on our journey to help us pivot onto our best path.

No matter who you are, protecting your energy allows you to make your greatest contribution to yourself and others. When you live your life fast by the ticking clock, you fall into the trap of reacting to crises and living by the expectations of others. Recalibrating your energy clock teaches you to live deliberately, with intention.

+ Can we lead if we are exhausted?
+ Can we get the results we want if we are distracted and unfocused?
+ Can we do meaningful work if our tanks are empty?
+ Can we inspire others if we aren't inspired ourselves?

I hate to break it to you, but *no*! Nothing will ever truly move forward if you are not investing *meaning* into how you spend your time. The purpose of the energy clock is to shift how you currently view your time to focus instead on where you invest your energy. This will in turn *create* more energy for you throughout your day.

In other words, it's about going to the end of our lives and careers and ensuring we can look back and know we put energy into what mattered most, because you know what the greatest tragedy in life is? Getting to the end of it all and realizing that we spent our energy on the wrong people and the wrong things.

This is not a book about time management or

productivity. This is not a book about not hitting goals or not aiming high. In fact, it's the very opposite. It is a book about how we can set our energy clocks to drive daily connection between where we spend our time and what matters most to us. It's about learning to manage our energy to move our lives forward with purpose, not just stay on schedule.

Setting our energy clock is simple, but it isn't easy. No matter your gender, age, level of wealth or education, skin color, ethnicity, or job title, you have an energy clock, and it's up to you to set it. You control your energy—no one else does.

In the hour it takes to read this book, you could change the rest of your life. Setting your energy clock will change your relationship with yourself and with others. It will change the way you lead at home and at work.

Because here's the truth: there are lots of things in life we can't control, but one thing we *can* control is where we put our energy.

PERFORMING AN ENERGY AUDIT

"Where your concentration goes, your energy flows, and that's what grows."

—TOM BRADY, NFL QUARTERBACK

TOM BRADY WILL GO DOWN AS ONE OF THE GREATEST NFL players in history. It's easy to credit Brady's success to his immense talent, but that would only tell a sliver of the story.

One of the big reasons for Brady's success is that he is intentional about managing all aspects of his energy.

Brady is known for his disciplined approach to health (the man considers avocado ice cream a treat) and fitness (hasn't missed a game due to injury in the last ten seasons), but he places an equal emphasis on the need to stay mentally focused and connected.

"When you play professional sports," Brady said in

a 2017 interview with Peter King, "you subject yourself to a lot of criticism. What I've learned from myself is I don't want to give my power away to other people by letting my own emotions be subjected to what their thoughts or opinions are. So if someone calls me something, that's their problem. It's not my problem. I'm not going to give away my power."

He understands that results aren't an accident, but a byproduct of a conscious decision: Where will I focus my energy?

Like Brady, great leaders ask this question too. So do great teams. They are intentional about who and what they give their energy to and why.

Compare your energy audit to the audits technicians run on heating and cooling systems—there is a balance for both functions to create efficiency. You might think of heat as the energy you need to get things done, and cooling as the energy replacement time (down time) needed in between those bursts of energy. Both are important, especially in avoiding burnout.

The importance of energy management is magnified in endurance sports, where athletes have to compete over extended time periods and long distances. It's what Olympic marathoner Steve Spence calls "managing your energy pie."

He remembers the advice that physiologist David Martin gave him during training: *There are always going to be runners who are faster than you. There will always be runners more talented than you, and runners who seem to be training harder than you. The key to beating them is to train harder and to learn how to most efficiently manage your energy pie.*

All the things that take time and energy make up your energy pie, and there's only so much room in the pie. What are the pieces that make up your energy pie? Do they all belong in the pie? Or do you need to make some changes?

For Spence, running was his priority. He made the tough decision to quit graduate school and run professionally. He went on to compete in the world championships and made the 1992 Olympic marathon team.

That's the major difference that refocusing our energy can have on our performance.

To set your energy clock, you must have the guts to ditch the things that don't bring meaning to your life. Invest more time in the things that sustain and replenish your energy and eliminate or better manage those things that drain your energy.

Meet a friend of mine. To protect his identity, let's call him Frank. Frank is a sales executive at a large pharmaceutical company. Every time I talk to him (particularly lately), he is always exhausted. He's more stressed, he says, than he has ever been at work. He has more to do than time to do it.

I can see it's affecting his home life too. He's shared about his wife of twenty years and their children he feels he is neglecting—especially a teenage daughter he snaps at more than he hugs.

"I am exhausted," he told me. "It's this client. It

won't last that long, maybe six more months tops, but I better get a raise and a nice bonus after this, that is for sure."

I knew that his promotion had come with no raise, only a promise of a bump later. Whenever later is.

"What are you chasing?" I asked him.

"What?" he said.

"What are you chasing?"

"What the hell do you mean?"

"Why are you putting all your energy into something that's clearly consuming you? Your health is slipping. You said your family is being compromised. What is the end goal? The raise?"

He looked down, then back up at me.

"I don't know."

Beyond being exhausted, my friend was clearly feeling confused and drained.

His wheels were turning as he began to recognize the unintended consequences of his actions.

AUDITING YOUR ENERGY

**"Make every day
your masterpiece."**
—JOHN WOODEN, BASKETBALL COACH

FOLLOWING THAT CONVERSATION, FRANK AGREED TO
do an energy audit with me.

An energy audit simply means looking holistically at all of your energy outputs and determining where you are gaining energy and where you are losing it. That awareness is the first step in creating change.

Frank needed the energy audit badly.

I believed he could make adjustments that would get him back on track, but we had to start with three basic questions.

First question: "What *increases* your energy and is meaningful to you?" I asked. "Let's start with some personal examples."

He perked up.

"Going for a run," he said. "I'm training for a 5K in March. Date nights with my wife, coaching my daughter Sarah's basketball team, and volunteering every Saturday morning through my church. Those are all the personal areas of my life when I feel energized and like I'm doing something that's meaningful."

I jotted his answers at the top of my page:

+ Running
+ Date nights
+ Coaching daughter's team
+ Volunteering

"What about at work?" I prompted him. "What are the things that bring you energy there?"

"Business-development opportunities," he said immediately. "I love prospecting new business, and I get excited every time I see a new opportunity evolve. My colleague Sam, he keeps me grounded and focused and knows how to shift my perspective when I'm having a bad day. I love working with him.

"Going out in the field… It might sound old-school, but I love the face-to-face contact with my customers and seeing firsthand what's going on in their practices, and I've been working on a new partnership with a well-respected hospital here locally that's going to really expand our market share, so that's got me excited."

I added those to his answers:

+ Being out in the field
+ Business development
+ Working with Sam
+ New hospital partnership

"What's in the middle?" I asked Frank next. "What are the things that don't necessarily increase or decrease your energy, but they exist? You need to accomplish them and keep them on your radar each week."

"I've been on the board of my neighborhood

association for a few years now, so that takes up time and energy. At work, managing my direct reports. I have five now, and I'm part of the team that's working on our rebranding and website launch."

I capture these too:

+ Board commitment
+ Managing direct reports
+ Rebranding and website launch

Lastly, I asked for the exact opposite. "What decreases your energy? Give me some personal examples first."

He paused. "Managing my kids' schedules—it's never ending," he said quickly. "And recently, my relationship with my best friend Jason. He's going through a divorce, and as much as I love him, the constant negativity and complaining is starting to get to me."

"And what about at work?" I asked. "What's draining your energy there?"

"Travel," Frank said, shaking his head. "I've been on the road three of the last four weeks and it's starting to take its toll. My relationship with my boss. I hate to say it, but I just dread going into the office when I know he's there. He always focuses on what we are not doing and never points out the good work we are doing… and then probably just the typical office drama. We are going through a lot of change in our sales process, and it's hasn't been an easy transition."

I wrote these down too:

+ Kids' schedules
+ Relationship with best friend
+ Work travel
+ Relationship with boss
+ Office drama
+ Change in sales process

To recap, the energy audit involves three simple questions.

 GREEN: What increases your energy and is meaningful to you?

 ORANGE: What are the things that don't necessarily increase or decrease your energy, but they exist?

 RED: What decreases your energy?

Now we could see what his choices were doing for him—and what they cost to his energy. So let's break it down further.

"OK, now tell me this: How do you feel when you are here?" I pointed to the green.

Frank lit up. "I feel ready to take on the world—optimistic, energized, focused. Like I'm doing things that matter."

"How often have you been feeling that way recently?" I asked.

"Rarely!" he said, staring at me. "*Very* rarely!"

"OK, now tell me this: How do you feel here?" I pointed to the red.

"Ugh…" he said. "I feel anxious, frustrated, and I know I am short with people. Tired. I get more defensive with my wife and people at work."

"OK, so tell me this: How often have you been feeling that way recently?"

"A lot. More than I want to, that is for damn sure."

"All of this is super normal," I reassured him. Every

feeling he was dealing with is shared by so many people. What this exercise has shown me in all of my years of working with athletes, coaches, leaders, and teams is that each area we've identified factors into our overarching emotions.

All day, every day, our energy ebbs and flows, often without us really realizing it until we either hit a high point or totally crash on the flip side. We could hang up the phone from some internal politics at work and be in the red. A few minutes later, we could close a deal and instantly be in the green. Or sometimes we are living in the orange, checking off items on our to do list with little thought. The point of the energy audit is to become much more aware of what's replenishing our energy and what is depleting it. By doing that, we can then become more intentional about who and what we give our energy to.

What I just walked Frank through is the first steps of an energy audit. Here's what it looks like when you put all the pieces together:

Example of Frank's chart:

MAXIMIZE

What increases your energy and is meaningful to you?

+ Running
+ Date nights
+ Coaching daughter's team
+ Volunteering
+ Being out in the field
+ Business development
+ Working with Sam
+ New hospital partnership

BE EFFICIENT

What doesn't necessarily increase or decrease your energy but exists?

• Board meetings
• Managing direct reports
• Rebranding launch

ELIMINATE OR MANAGE

What decreases your energy?

− Kids' schedules
− Relationship with my best friend
− Work travel
− Relationship with boss
− Office drama
− Change in sales process

It's about knowing where we are and how to shift our energy toward the green—our energizers—as much as possible. In sum, we want to:

1 *Maximize* our energizers.

2 Be more *efficient* with everything in-between.

3 *Eliminate* or *manage* our drainers.

We will dig into that further when we talk about setting our energy clock.

MAXIMIZE YOUR ENERGIZERS

"The best way to make your dreams come true is to wake up."

—PAUL VALÉRY, POET

FRANK WAS STARTING TO SEE THE POWER OF THE energy audit. I suggested that we go back and look at that sweet spot, the green.

"*Why* do those activities and priorities really matter to you?" I asked him.

"Well, running matters to me because it's when I think," he explained. "I sort of escape, and I feel like I'm making progress toward an important goal—improving my health. And Friday date nights with my wife matter to me, because when we connect, I really feel whole. I love coaching my daughter's team, because it's our time together doing something we both love, and

28

I value what she learns from competing on a team. And then volunteering with my church keeps things in perspective. It reminds me that my problems really aren't that big, and it helps to shift my focus to others."

"With work, I love being out in the field and the business-development opportunities, because it gives me a chance to see the impact my work actually makes instead of being cooped up in the office crunching numbers."

He clearly knew what he needed. Now came the buy-in. "Which of these energizers in green can you schedule more of in your life?"

"I could run more," he said. "Like three times a week. I maybe get one run in a week now."

"OK, cool, when? Morning? Night? What days are best for this?"

"Sunday afternoon for sure works. I have a standing conference call every Monday, Wednesday, and Friday, so I just never know those days. So let's say Sunday, Tuesday, and Thursday."

"OK, what would be an easy way to ensure this happens? Let's think about a way to make it a priority by protecting the time on your schedule, and it may mean enlisting people who could help you with this, like an assistant, family member, or friend."

He didn't have to think very long.

"I just need to hold the weekday runs in my calendar so my assistant doesn't schedule any early morning meetings," he said. "And for the Sunday afternoon run, I can ask my wife for support. Actually, she'll be excited, because she wants me to lose twenty pounds, so that won't be a problem!"

"So right now, on your calendar, could you go out a few weeks and block these out?"

"Yes."

"And tomorrow when you go in, could you share this with your assistant so she is aware that on Tuesday and Thursday mornings there will be no more 7:00 a.m. breakfast meetings?"

"Yes."

"And your wife, when could you ask her?"

"Tonight. I actually can't wait to share this with her."

"Cool. So by late morning tomorrow, you could have a new system in place to protect your runs, right?"

"Yep." He smiled. I literally heard him exhale.

"OK, want to keep going?"

We dug into the rest of what energized him personally—his green zone. I watched his body language change. It was like he could see the light at the end of the tunnel again.

"You know what is cool about this?" Frank commented. "We're talking about personal energizers, but I'll be better at work because of this."

"OK, let's hit your green zone at work. Want to talk about business development?"

"Sure."

"How often does this show up in your world now?"

"Not enough. Just ask my boss!" he laughs. "You

see, I get pulled into conference calls and meetings, and when I finally come up for air, my email inbox is full."

"Do you really need to be on all the calls and at all the meetings?"

"Ahh, no chance. I'd say I should be in 60 percent of them."

"OK. And your boss wants you doing more business development, right?"

"*Yes!*"

"What is at risk to tally up the amount of time you spend in an average week on these calls and in these meetings and then sit with your boss and discuss how you can cut back there to *maximize* your time on business development?"

"Nothing is at risk. In fact, he would be pumped."

Frank quickly calculated that he spent on average about eight hours per week on unnecessary calls and meetings—time he could devote to business development. He started rattling off with excitement what he could do with those eight hours from a business-development perspective and even his short list of relationships he wants to cultivate.

"When can you meet with your boss?"

"Tuesday. We already have a standing meeting every Tuesday. I'll do it then."

"One last thing—I want you to block off time in your calendar specifically for business development once you get the unnecessary calls and meetings off your schedule. Protect this time you have captured, so it doesn't get sucked away by something else that is less important to you."

What my friend discovered is something you can apply to your own life. Become clear and intentional about what gives you energy, and find ways to support and protect that time. Scheduling and systems are critical to feed what gives you energy.

When we do this, we will gradually spend less time in the other colors. We will put more importance on the things that matter most—the green zone.

BE EFFICIENT

"Begin with the end in mind."
—STEPHEN COVEY, AUTHOR

SO WHAT ABOUT THE THINGS FRANK IDENTIFIED IN THE orange? These are the things that Frank deals with on a regular basis. They don't necessarily energize him, but they also aren't depleting his energy.

What you've identified in the orange is where you can simply be more efficient. You don't have a problem here, but you aren't really reaping any rewards either.

So this is one area where, typically, you can and should be more efficient—not just physically, but mentally and emotionally as well. The orange is the zone that can easily be a trap if you aren't paying attention. If you aren't careful, you can find yourself quickly slipping from orange to red, which quickly becomes problematic. But if you are intentional, orange can also be an opportunity to lift up to the green. Efficiency and awareness are the key here.

For Frank, that meant remaining on his association board for another year but dropping off the planning committee, which was the part of his board commitment that consumed most of his energy.

It meant streamlining the way he communicated with his direct reports by scheduling weekly check-in calls on Monday mornings and setting clearer expectations to minimize the amount of clarifying questions that trailed on after these conversations. It also meant establishing a new rule where all of Frank's direct reports committed to attempting to solve any issues directly with the other person before coming to him with the problem. That not only cut down on the energy Frank had to invest in unnecessary meetings; it also empowered his team to have tough conversations themselves, which is an important skill in sales.

And as for the rebranding project, it was short-term and was needed for the company's growth.

Frank realized he had been getting worked up over it for the wrong reasons when, in fact, the rebranding was going to help him with a lot of his business-development opportunities. So Frank pulled back and gave his project team clear goals and objectives that they needed to accomplish. But instead of getting involved on the technical side—which always left him confused and frustrated—Frank left that up to the design team. "Be efficient with where you spend your energy," he reminded himself. He needed to be involved, but not in every aspect of the project.

MANAGE YOUR DRAINERS

"You only live once, but if you do it right, once is enough."

—MAE WEST, ACTRESS

THE RED IS WHERE MOST PEOPLE STRUGGLE TO MAKE change. This is where we want to eliminate energy drains wherever we can and manage them better where we cannot.

So once you get to your red zone, you should always ask yourself two follow-up questions.

1   Is this something I can eliminate?

2   If not, how can I better manage my energy around it?

Let's use the examples Frank gave and see how he handled it.

Frank and his wife both work demanding jobs, and it felt like coming home to a second job for both of them when it came to managing their three kids' schedules. It was a necessary but not-so-fun part of parenting that was sucking the energy out of both Frank and his wife.

So how could Frank better manage his energy around it? Part of the problem was that no one seemed to know who needed to be where, when. So Frank and his wife set up a family Google calendar. They sat down with their kids and entered all the extracurriculars, like after-school tutoring sessions, sports schedules, and sleepovers at friends' houses. "If it's not in the calendar, it's not our problem," Frank told his kids, only partly joking.

It was a good exercise in responsibility for their children who were old enough to start prioritizing for themselves too. Two unexpected but awesome outcomes resulted from the conversation. Their oldest son volunteered to drive his younger brother to soccer practice after school on Tuesdays and Thursdays, and their daughter Sarah admitted that she actually dreaded drama practice and would rather spend her time elsewhere, which freed up the schedule.

Frank's relationship with his best friend Jason, who was going through a divorce, was also draining him unnecessarily. But was it something he could simply eliminate? No, he didn't want to do that. This was his best friend since college, and in his heart he knew it was just a rough patch!

We all have relationships in our lives that can drain our energy, but that doesn't mean we need to go cutting off people right and left. Sure, sometimes a relationship is really toxic and that might be the necessary action, but more often than not we just need to get better about not giving it so much emotional energy.

For Frank, that started with reframing his narrative. Instead of telling himself *Ugh, here goes Jason calling me again*, Frank consciously shifted to gratitude. *This is my best friend in the whole world, and he trusts me enough to confide in me during what must be an incredibly difficult time for him personally. If I can help him keep perspective while he goes through this divorce, maybe I can help him continue to show up and be a great dad to his kids instead of getting frustrated and checking out.*

Just that simple mental shift allows Frank to reframe his energy drain in a positive manner. He's shifting from the red zone to the orange. By focusing on better communication and simply reframing their relationship, he's eliminated some of the anxiety he felt every time Jason called. If Jason called when Frank was already in the red zone, instead of answering and getting more annoyed, he now just asked if he could call him back later that day or meet over the weekend, when he could give Jason the attention he needed. By doing that, he found himself actually listening and finding ways to help Jason shift from blaming to solutions, instead of counting the minutes they'd been on the phone!

What about work travel? For Frank, that meant

a few things, but the biggest factor was in bringing *green* to the *red*. What do I mean by that?

While Frank hated being on flights all day, he actually loved exploring other cities. The problem was, he was usually so drained by the travel and work commitments that he ended up holed up in the hotel all day when he had free time.

So instead, Frank looked at his work travel for the upcoming four weeks. He would be in San Diego with an extra day in between travel, which he had been annoyed by. However, now he realized he could get a tee time at the course there that he'd been dying to play but never actually booked.

And what about the following week when he had a Friday meeting in New York? Frank wasn't a big fan of New York City, but his kids had never been. What if he extended the stay and made it a weekend trip where his kids and wife could join?

And what if on his flight he finished that book he'd been complaining he never got the chance to read?

As he looked at his travel schedule with fresh eyes, Frank was excited about the *green* shining through.

Sometimes energy drains are obvious, like a toxic relationship, but energy drains can also simply be distractions that aren't serving our purpose and are taking us off course. Those are often more difficult to spot, unless you audit your energy consistently. Energy drains—like energy builders—are unique for us all. A long commute through traffic may drain most of us, but for a young mom on the go, it could be her designated quiet time each day to focus on her own goals and plan for the day. The important thing is to look at your personal energy audit and create a path for yourself that rewards your personal energy builders. The more competing demands we have on our time, the more difficult it becomes to manage our energy, unless we are intentional.

The key about the red zone is knowing that we can't eliminate everything, but when we can, we should, and when we can't, we must recognize how to let the green shine through. But sometimes the energy drains that show up in the red are things that really require our attention or are important to us.

That's where we want to ask ourselves, *How can I better manage my energy around this?* Sometimes that means asking for support. Other times it's learning how to make sure you don't give it unnecessary emotional energy.

The energy audit is a powerful tool, because it gives you a baseline and helps develop awareness about how your choices affect your energy. Without that awareness, you can't possibly make the necessary changes.

We can do an energy audit as an individual (like I did with Frank), as a team (that includes families), and as an organization.

For example, with my own team, we do a quarterly energy audit.

I'll ask each direct report what takes them to the green, orange, and red. As a leader, you can better position your team for success when you know what each person enjoys, tolerates, and hates, and then you can expand it to the team or organization: Collectively, where are we losing energy and where are we gaining it?

To pull it all together:

1   What increases your energy and is meaningful to you?

    ▸   How can you *maximize* and invest in these?

2   What are the things that don't necessarily increase or decrease your energy, but they exist?

    ▸   How can you be more *efficient* here?

3   What decreases your energy?

    ▸   Is it something you can *eliminate*? Then eliminate it.

    ▸   If not, how can you better *manage* your energy here?

The energy audit is powerful. It's collaborative. It's clarifying. It's transparent. It's downright healthy.

Do you think after that simple exercise, your team is more or less likely to stay together and win together? Do you think at the end of that simple exercise, your team would be more or less connected? Or what about your family? Powerful, right?

We all deal with people, places, systems, and events that drain our energy. The important thing is to recognize that *you* control your energy—how you spend it, where it goes, and how to best allocate it.

YOU CAN NEVER DO IT ALL

"You can have it all, just not all at once."

—MARY WEST, MY MOM

WE LIVE IN A WORLD WHERE WE ARE TOLD WE CAN *DO* *it all.* However, we can't—or rather, it depends on how you define *all.* We have to make choices and determine what matters most in order to prioritize our energy.

It's tragic when the thing that *takes* isn't what matters most to you. We've seen it over and over. The high-level executive climbs the ladder only to realize his or her family is falling apart. Or in my work as a sports agent, an athlete racks up so many accolades that he or she can no longer separate who they are as a person from what they do for a living.

These are common stories, right? But they are heartbreaking.

What I hope this book helps you with is to put your time and energy toward things that are most meaningful to you—and it starts with awareness.

Let's get to work.

PART

2

SEEKING THE IMPORTANT

HAVE YOU EVER FOUND YOURSELF IN A SITUATION AND thought, *Why am I doing this?*

+ Why did I say yes?
+ Why am I in this meeting?
+ Why are we (fill in the *we*—our family, our team) doing this?

Maybe your team is deep in a project, and you peek at your annual goals only to realize that *all this work isn't aligned with our organization's goals*.

Or you are in a meeting you need to be in. You want to be in it, but you are exhausted from doing the things that *don't* matter to you. Those things rob you of your energy and, as a result, you now don't have enough for the things that *do* matter to you.

Ever try to squeeze in "just one more thing" in a day? Or before a call?

Ever rush through a meeting agenda in order to try to get to the next meeting on time—cutting out the creative dialogue and making the whole thing a waste? Ever miss your kids all day, but then lose your patience with them when you come home, because you're still thinking about a bad moment at work?

Ever wish you had more energy for the things that matter most to you, and that you could spend less energy on the things that don't?

Does that ever happen? All the time, right? I know.

I get it. I've been there and still find myself there at times.

+ *But Molly, I can't help it.*
+ *But my boss…*
+ *But my client…*
+ *But my kids…*

Zip it. Those are all excuses. *You* control your energy.

+ *But Molly, I am not in control of my time.*

Exactly. Most of us aren't in total control of our time. But we *are* in control of our energy. We are in control of what we tell ourselves and how we react in these moments, which is all the more reason to set your energy clock so you can navigate these moments better.

Most of us are tied to our calendars, our watches, our smart phones. We have time-based alerts popping up on our phones and computers constantly. It's five minutes until… Well, Siri reminds us of *when*.

It's time to ask yourself two words: *For what?*

And four more: What are you chasing?

Why are you racing around to the next activity, to the next unfulfilling obligation? Why are you exhausted from all the busyness—*what's it all for?*

Sit with that for a moment! And while you're at it, ask yourself what's happening in your circle of influence.

+ Why is your team scattered?
+ Why are mistakes being made?
+ Why are there unfinished projects?
+ Who are your choices affecting?
+ What's at risk because of your behaviors?
+ How is your journey impacting others?

Now imagine the end of your life. It's your ninetieth birthday party. Who is in the room? Where are you? What are they saying? What do you want them to be saying?

Or just as effective, imagine what you want people to say about you at your retirement party at the end of your career.

She was brave...authentic...motivating...solution-oriented...committed...loving...forgiving...she really listened...

Wow, that sounds a lot better than:

She was always exhausted and distracted... I never felt like she was really there... She was always running from one thing to the next...

Or skip the retirement party and cut to the real bottom line. What do you want your tombstone to say?

My friend Tiffany Dufu, author of *Drop the Ball*, told me what she *doesn't* want: "I don't want it to say, 'She got a lot of stuff done.'"

So why do we act so busy and rushed and frantic in our daily lives? Because we aren't seeing the big picture.

Sometimes it takes the end of life for that picture to crystallize for us, but we can get that clarity sooner.

"Meditate on your mortality" is the wise advice from Ryan Holiday, author of *The Obstacle Is the Way*.

Too often in life, it takes a crisis for us to wake up and pay attention to the effect of our choices. My hope in writing this book is that you'll realize sooner the power you have when you take control of your energy.

Here's the struggle: we get confused about what matters most.

Here's a big glass of truth: the reward isn't in the results; it's in the journey.

When we don't seek what matters most to us, we can find ourselves wildly off course. At the end of achieving our asses off, we think it's going to be great...and it's not.

When we get to that thing we thought we were chasing—the promotion, the money, the fancy car, the big house—we feel empty, because none of this is ever enough.

This is a lesson usually learned the hard way. A

few years ago, my mom flew down from Michigan to help with our daughters, because I had a busy travel week with multiple speaking engagements. In addition, there was an "optional" board meeting on my calendar that I felt obligated to attend in Miami. That meeting added two nights to my already packed schedule, right in the middle of two keynotes.

As I landed for the not-required-but-feeling-obligated meeting, I felt so empty. Just awful. I missed my girls and husband and thought, *I don't really have to be here.* I called my mom in tears. She reassured me the girls were fine, but I wasn't. I was still crying when I called my husband. I needed to reset my energy clock for the short term; I needed to reconnect with what fulfilled me. Luckily, there was still time to adjust.

I went to only part of the optional meeting. I rearranged flights so I could spend a day at home before heading to my next speaking engagement. I landed in Atlanta at 9:30 a.m., hustled home, and dropped off my bags. Then I headed to our girls' school and surprised my daughters. I checked in the front office and walked into their lunch room where they were eating. They lit up.

"Mom, I thought you weren't going to be home today?"

"I wasn't, baby, but surprise! I am now. After lunch, do you want to scoot for ice cream and an afternoon at the park? It's beautiful outside."

"What?"

"I already talked to your teachers. They said it was fine."

We had a blast. Ice cream. Picnic. Conversation. The beautiful weather made it feel like it was meant to be. We spent that afternoon and evening together before I had to get back on the airplane—but this time I left with a full heart and clear head.

Two nights later, I returned home determined to come up with a new process to avoid this scenario in the future. I created a system with my internal team for managing the number of keynotes I committed to weekly. I created clarity as to what to say yes and no to, and I asked my husband to help me weed out the not-required-but-feeling-obligated requests. He's always been my sounding board, and it's so important to have this kind of support for the journey.

These moments happen to all of us at some point in our lives. We can't beat ourselves up every time, but the important thing is to make sure it's the exception and not the rule. A friend of mine who leads a large team at a Fortune 100 company has two children. His son is a great baseball player, but he rarely made his games, because he was either traveling or working late at the office. One day, he told me he arrived in the bottom of the fifth inning only to be greeted by other parents saying, "Did you see it?" In the fourth inning, his son hit a grand slam to take the team up 4–0, and it was the first one of his life. His dad missed it. He missed the moment, and sadly he had missed others, big and small. When his son asked him if he got the video on his phone, it sank in.

That night when he got home, he inputted his son's baseball schedule into his calendar. He attempted to move the things that could be moved that overlapped his son's games and set a reminder in his calendar to get next season's calendar right when it came out so he could offset missing other big moments.

Bottom line: *Until you get clear on what's most important, your decisions around your energy will not be optimal.*

As teams and as organizations, we need clarity, focus, and accountability as we seek the important. The more success you have, the easier it is to become scattered and to do the unimportant. It's easier to say we are *busy* than to admit that we might actually be unproductive and even chasing the wrong stuff.

Now zoom in for a moment. I've been talking about the big picture, but inside of moments, we must also ask ourselves, *What do I want most?*

This is a question I try to ask myself inside of critical conversations and decisions. Sometimes when we ask ourselves this simple question, it reframes the way we will handle the situation, even as it unfolds around and in front of us.

For example, if a client is sharing frustration about something that didn't get done, we feel our emotions rise. The defensiveness and reactivity are natural.

But right then, pause. *What do I want most? To fix the mistake? A happy client? Connection? Alignment?* Either way you slice it, I bet it changes your conversation.

We need to manage our energy with this question front and center: *What do I want most?*

People who embrace the ways of the energy clock know when it is set and when it isn't set. Here's how:

THE **ENERGY CLOCK** MODEL

	WHEN YOUR **ENERGY CLOCK** IS SET...	WHEN YOUR **ENERGY CLOCK** IS *NOT* SET...
YOU BELIEVE...	You have the energy for what matters most	You don't have the time for what matters most
YOU FEEL...	Energized Fulfilled Focused Connected	Exhausted Unfulfilled Distracted Disconnected
YOU...	Anticipate Maintain healthy accountability Stay curious	React Blame and complain Behave defensively

When you can answer *What do I want most?* in the middle of an opportunity or crisis and align your energy with your values, you are setting the energy clock for yourself.

ELIMINATING THE DRAINS

"They always say time changes things, but you actually have to change them yourself."

—ANDY WARHOL, ARTIST

OFTEN THE BIGGEST ENERGY DRAINER IS RESISTING change. *Fighting it.* Battling it.

Maybe you're faced with adapting to a new system at work. Or it's one of those personal changes we know we need to make that we have been resisting. Or it's even something we know would benefit our team at work, but we haven't pulled back long enough to lead the change that would make a positive difference.

When you resist change, you're spending your energy staying in one place. Do you really think that's a good idea?

So, let's dig into how we embrace change, how we lean into it. That's how we set ourselves up to believe that changing our mindset—and putting our energy against our most fulfilling activities—will better serve us and those around us.

For example, do you ever look down at your phone and see the name on the phone and say to yourself, *Ohhh mmmyyyy... What do they want?*

And in the moment, there's that deflation when you feel the energy sort of rush out of your body. You look at the name and think, *I just don't have it in me to deal with this person right now*. It's so easy to hit decline, isn't it?

And they are gone and you instantly feel better—but only for a moment. Until they call back, or you meet with them, or your inbox starts blowing up.

I had a client like this. She called me a few times a day, and every time I felt like I couldn't fill her cup, *ever*!

Finally I asked myself, *Is she better than her problems?* In other words, *Is she worth all this energy?*

Meanwhile I had a team of agents who were managing and recruiting athletes, coaches, and broadcasters.

They needed my energy. I had other clients. *They needed my energy.* I had other support people. *They needed my energy.* Not to mention, her calls came at night and on weekends too, so surely it was flowing into my family time. *They need my energy.*

What is at risk if I make a change and let this relationship go?

It's not an easy move in a business that values and sustains relationships, because there are actually more agents than athletes to represent—all relationships in this industry are at a premium, but not every relationship is worth the energy it takes. Finally, I mustered the strength to have a difficult conversation and what came from that was the clarity that I needed to let it go.

Phew! Wow! I discovered that the amount of energy I was giving that relationship was more than I ever imagined. Now I had the capacity to give to the clients where there was more alignment, which was making great clients even better.

In this situation, I could give more energy to the agents who needed support managing and recruiting talent. Now that I wasn't getting sucked into her unreasonable demands, I could focus on serving clients.

The bottom line was that this change was personally and professionally transformative. Now, of course that isn't always the right solution for every situation, to put a stop to a relationship. The point is that it takes courage to change. Sometimes it feels safer to stay where we are than to risk the unknown. Change is at the heart of the energy clock. It's how it works. Change is the world we live in. It's why we need the energy clock, because life is fluid and sometimes we can spend so much energy staying in place when we could shift our energy elsewhere with greater results.

The truth is we can change, and we can control where we invest our energy. The best are constantly auditing their energy, pivoting as needed, to stay focused on the question:

Is there change needed to align with what I want most—with what is meaningful and gives me and those who matter most my best energy?

BE WHERE YOUR FEET ARE

"If you must look back, do so forgivingly.
If you must look forward, do so prayerfully.
However, the wisest thing you can do is to
be present in the present. Gratefully. "

—MAYA ANGELOU, POET

IF YOU STAY PRESENT, YOU CAN STAY DIALED IN ON what's important. As Alabama football coach Nick Saban constantly reminds his players, "Be where your feet are."

I love this way of putting it, because it's literally grounding you where you are, and that's what being present does. It grounds you in the moment.

There are lots of things in life we can't control and plenty we *can* control. Knowing the distinction can make a huge difference in energy management.

I think of this like an outer circle and an inner circle. The outer circle are the things I can't control—the uncontrollable. The inner circle contains things I *can* control. The things that need my energy. Where my energy makes the biggest difference.

The best athletes do this really well. Golfers won't look at the scoreboard on the back nine, because they can only control their play. Tennis players like Serena Williams don't look at the draw in advance, because they want to stay focused on the present moment. They control what they can control. The rest is just noise.

Coaches love to say to players, "Do your job."

In other words, avoid getting lost in distractions and stay focused on what matters—what you can control. How does this really show up for you? Look at your energy audit. There are so many things in the boxes that we can't control, right?

Managing our energy around the uncontrollable is a key component of energy management.

✦ I can't control other people's opinions of me, but I can control whether I let them affect me.

+ I can't control that a sales person didn't close a deal, but I can control my response—how I show up and support him, coach him, lead him to better his odds for the next close.

+ I can't control that my client is late to our meeting, but I can control my attitude when he does show up.

Now let's look at what's in your circles.

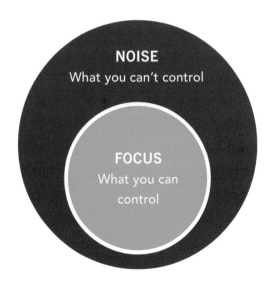

In the inner circle, write down the things you can control in your life. This is where you should focus. Here are some thought-starters:

+ Attitude	+ Beliefs
+ Effort	+ Values
+ Mindset	+ Perspective
+ Choices	+ Response
+ Actions	+ Energy!

In the outer circle, write the things you can't control in your life. This is noise. Here are some thought-starters, but don't forget to review your energy audit as well for some ideas:

+ Other people	+ Gender/race/age
+ Circumstances	+ The past
+ Opinions	+ Results

A key component to managing our energy clock is focusing on what we can control and not investing our energy in things we have no control over. Why get worked up, upset, and resistant to something we know we have no control over?

For an athlete, awareness might mean not letting a ref's bad call bother them during the heat of the game. For an executive, it might be recognizing moments that they shouldn't invest energy in—an employee's attitude in a meeting or a naysayer's opinion.

It means asking *what can we control inside of this moment?*

What *can* we control if we have an employee with a bad attitude? How about a one-on-one meeting with them to discuss after the meeting to get to the root of the behavior?

What about a naysayer's opinion? Consider the source, and whether there might be some truth to it. Based on those two things, you might actually learn a valuable lesson from it or open up meaningful dialogue—otherwise, disregard it.

The point is there are lots of things we have control over. Focusing on what we *can't* control is just a waste of our energy.

When we allow uncontrollables to deplete our energy, there's a bad side effect. That usually brings down the energy of those around us too.

BEING PRESENT IS ESSENTIAL

"The most we can hope for is to create the best possible conditions for success, then let go of the outcome. The ride is a lot more fun that way."

—PHIL JACKSON, BASKETBALL COACH

I LOVE THE SAYING: *DON'T CONFUSE ACTIVITY WITH* *accomplishment.* That's a mistake we can often make. Busy is addictive.

But the key is pausing inside of busy and asking if the behavior aligns with where we want to put our energy. It's checking our energy clock and adjusting as needed. If we find that we feel we can't be present at home, in meetings, or at the office, it's likely because we aren't acting in our best interests. We're not acting like essentialists, as Greg McKeown defines it.

The author of *Essentialism*, McKeown talks about focusing on what is most important and removing the rest. When we do this it is much easier to be present. We have less coming at us.

Our society makes us think *more is better.* But in believing so, we've bought into a lie. We can't do it all; we can't have it all, and are we even sure that's really what we want? We have to get clear on *who and what deserves our energy and why.* McKeown points out that most things aren't essential, so we have to shift our mindset and start the hard work of focusing our energy on what is, in fact, essential.

Being present is anchored in discipline. It's hanging up the phone on our way into our house so we can be present when we circle up with the people in our lives who matter most. It's the ability to maintain eye contact—not screen contact—during meetings so we can be focused and connected to our teams. It's going on date nights and family outings without devices, or putting them on silent in our pockets or purses, so we can give our full selves to the finite time we have for the people who are most important to us.

Did you know that the mere presence of a cell phone can be distracting? That's right. A recent study in the *Journal of the Association for Consumer Research* found that a smartphone can demand its user's attention even when the person isn't using it or consciously thinking about it. Its mere presence impacts us. So it certainly affects the person sitting across the table from you!

Use technology to reinforce discipline, not undermine it. Make Siri remind you to put your phone away. Weird, right? But, hey! If it works, do what works. It might be sticky notes to remind us to just show up, to lock in and be present.

Being present is so important, because people can tell when we are. They can tell if we are checked out, somewhere else in our minds or wherever we happen to be scrolling. Our clients can tell, our families can tell, our employees can tell, and when we are present, we send a powerful message—a message that says *you really matter to me.*

Right now, it's all about *you.*

There's no stronger message that a leader can send. There's no better decision than to align your energy with your present moment. It's the only moment any of us have.

Here's an example. It wasn't a normal Friday, that is for sure. I was at my OB doctor to confirm I was, in fact, pregnant (only five months after delivering our first). Not only was a I pregnant, I was pregnant with twins. Miracles in the making, and already at 12.5 weeks. As I laid on the table in my doctor's office, and my husband and I peeled the shock off our faces like a face mask, I thought, *What time is it?* I looked down at my watch. It was 12:15 p.m. I had a 12:30 p.m. lunch with a client, NBA coach Doc Rivers, twenty minutes away.

"I have to go," I said to my doctor, rapidly grabbing my stuff to get moving down the hall.

"Well, Molly," she said as we walked, "you are a

high-risk pregnancy with multiples, so I will need to see you every other week."

That stopped me in my tracks. "Wait, what? Every other week? How does that work? Do you come to my house?"

She smiled, "No, you come here. Every other week."

"OK, you got it...but wow."

As I walked into the meeting with Doc carrying this

extra load (literally), all I could think about was how big this was, how my schedule was going to change, how I was going to need help, and the thousands of other logistical and emotional responses a person can have to being told they are fostering two new souls. I thought, *I need to park this and pick this up in an hour. Doc needs to talk about Doc, I need to be present for this meeting.* I remember walking into lunch and thinking:

I need to park this (TWINS!!!)
I need to park this (TWINS! This is a miracle!)
I can pick it up after this meeting (TWINS!)
But right now I need to be with Doc (twins!)
Be where your feet are (twins…)
Be present (twins.)
Be here.

Moments into the meeting, twins stopped being an interrupting thought. Despite flooring both myself and my family, the meeting was successful, and I told Doc the news a week later. Eventually, all the logistics of twins were settled too, and we could focus on the miracle of our girls.

We all have moments like these—big and small—and being present can be hard. However, all of us can tell when people are present and with us or if they are not. And, guess what, it matters. People are worth it—period. So how about a pregnant pause (get it?) before moments we know we need to be present, so we can put our energy into that moment—that's what matters most.

Even without life-altering news like twins, being present is easier said than done. Keeping up with the day-to-day drama can be enough to derail us completely from being present, in the moment, and engaged in our lives. Sometimes we need to come out of the "grind" and see ourselves from a new place. When we need to gain a bit of perspective, it's time to *zoom out.*

I remember moments in my career as a sports agent when coaches would get fired, players got released, or agents signed or lost a piece of business. Time and time again, I was thinking that each situation was such a big, big deal. We all find ourselves in these moments, don't we?

The truth is we get consumed thinking our world, our teams, our business, and our families are the center and the world is turning around us. Candidly, this is self-absorbed thinking, isn't it? If we could pause and zoom out, we would see how big these big deals really are within our own life and, even more, to the world. Instead of letting all these big problems dictate our stress and time, what if we shifted our perspective to realize that life, the world, and others will all carry on no matter what? Ask yourself: *Will this matter to me next year? Will I even remember this in five? Will anyone outside of myself even care about this next week?*

Perspective matters. Zoom out and check yourself from time to time. Perspective helps us serve others even better, as well as be present.

MINIMIZE THE DISTRACTIONS

"One way to boost our willpower and focus is to manage our distractions instead of letting them manage us."

—DANIEL GOLEMAN, AUTHOR

DISTRACTIONS ARE EVERYWHERE, AND IT'S SO EASY to engage with them without thinking. I saw this in full throttle with the athletes I represented.

Each time their phone rings, someone wants something—autographs, appearances, speaking engagements, money, you name it. When your name is on the back of a jersey and you make seven figures, your phone rings. There are so many opportunities to make more money, meet more people, feel more important—and lose time and energy.

It was my role to bring them back to the question:

What do you want most? What matters most? At that point in their lives, it's maximizing the short window of time they had in their career to set themselves up for the future.

For a baseball player, it is making sure they aren't getting pulled into too many off-field obligations and then don't have the energy needed to execute on the field.

For a golfer, it might be passing up the extra money for a paid outing to ensure they are fully prepared for the next tournament.

For a business person, it might be saying no to the unnecessary business lunch or the conference call that they really don't need to be on (because the whole time they will be muted and on email anyway) so they can lock in on the ones that do matter.

Distractions add up. Over time they can destroy us if we aren't locked in on what matters most.

Here's the truth: Distractions lead to multitasking. Multitasking is another word for a habit *guaranteed* to drain you.

Do me a favor for a moment. Try to verbalize directions to your children's school while writing the alphabet. You can't do it? Neither could I.

"Multitasking with digital technology is becoming even more commonplace in people of all generations than it was just a few years ago. All of us should be concerned," wrote L. Mark Carrier, Larry D. Rosen, and Jeffrey N. Rokkum, who conducted two of the largest studies on how people from different generations multitask, from Baby Boomers to the iGeneration.

Cognitive psychologists have long known about basic limitations in our psychological architecture. Perceptual constraints, central bottlenecks, and motor restrictions prevent people from carrying out multiple tasks at once. Certain tasks (like directions and the alphabet) can't be combined for multitasking. You can't switch between tasks without consequences.

Identify your distractions and you will be on your way to focusing your undiluted energy on what really matters most to you.

SHIFT PERSPECTIVE

**"Never let the fear of striking out
keep you from playing the game"**

—BABE RUTH, BASEBALL PLAYER

YOU CAN GET ENERGY BACK BY SHIFTING YOUR perspective.

I couldn't control the fact that I was one of the only female sports agents in the industry. There were lots of moments where I could have viewed being a female as a disadvantage or, for that matter, stressful—because it was.

Standing behind the dugout at batting practice, players were coming to talk to me and managers yelled at them for "hitting on that chick." Or at PGA Tour events, I'd be waiting on the practice range or standing behind my player's bags before a practice round, and I'd hear another player ask my guys, "Who is that chick?" My players always had my back—"That's my agent. Chill."

It was *chick*. All. The. Time.

But I reframed my narrative as a positive. The story I tried to tell myself, and sometimes it wasn't easy, was *What a gift. I am different.*

What a gift, I thought, *All these people will remember me, and what a gift that the players had my back.* I believe in these moments, the story I told myself helped me get clear on how and why I could achieve what I most wanted.

Because I believed that being a woman was a differentiator in a tough, tough profession and that my gender was a gift, I could represent athletes in a way that was very different than the male agents I competed against.

I actually could represent an entire family. I could support their wives and children as much as the athletes themselves. When a baseball player gets traded, he gets on the next airplane and his wife is standing there with a house, kids, and no husband. He's off and running, maybe even pitching the next day. She needed help. I built a team to support these moments.

This narrative led to other gifts. I was so young when I entered this profession. I could have gotten chewed up and spit out so easily. Instead, my story helped lead me to be my authentic self always. Or strive to, anyway, and that was so important.

Our narrative inside of good and challenging moments is one we often believe. When we shift our perspective and reframe what we tell ourselves, it helps us set our energy clock.

BE GENTLE ON YOURSELF

"Understanding the difference between healthy striving and perfectionism is critical to laying down the shield and picking up your life."

—BRENÉ BROWN, AUTHOR

PERFECTIONISM IS ANOTHER THING THAT WILL DRAIN your energy rapidly.

Failure is integral to succeeding at what you most want. That's what I observed over and over with the athletes and coaches that I represented. Baseball players knew that the only time they batted 1.000 was their first few plate appearances, if that. A team or athlete's ability to recover quickly from adversity is the difference between good and great.

Most great teams are solidified in moments of adversity. Clemson football coach Dabo Swinney has

led his team to two national championships, but before they got their first title, they suffered a heartbreaking defeat. After an undefeated regular season in 2015 (perfection!), Clemson lost to Alabama in the national championship game.

Dabo made sure that it was going to be a teachable moment. In the locker room, he stood in front of his players and gave them this message: "Don't let failure define you; let it develop you." He assured them they would be back the next season if they could do that.

And in a storybook ending, that's exactly what happened. A year later, Clemson again faced Alabama with a national championship on the line. This time, it ended in a victory for Dabo and his team.

When you're focused on perfection, you're not doing the work of becoming resilient. You're not spending energy on becoming good at moving forward from a mistake.

When perfectionists put their energy toward things

they can't control, it ends in disaster. Great coaches recognize that there are so many factors they cannot control—whether their players avoid injury, whether they end up in the right bracket or schedule, and whether the breaks go their way.

The best don't waste energy chasing perfection as defined by anyone else. They put their energy toward winning more often than they lose.

Embracing imperfection allows you to accept more risk. This is the way we grow. Perfectionism leads to a fixed mindset, and it keeps us from tapping our courage to change. A popular TED Talk by Reshma Saujani, the founder of Girls Who Code, makes the point that when we raise children to be perfect, we are not encouraging them to be brave.

Taking risks is the soul of innovation. "We have to begin to undo the socialization of perfection," Reshma says.

Humans aren't perfect, and we aren't meant to be. If we are going to try to change in life, if we are going to be curious to evolve, along that journey we will miss, we will fail, we will fall. It's OK.

Be gentle. Love yourself, and keep going. Be graceful to yourself. Speak to yourself like you would speak to someone you loved and respected.

Expect the unexpected, and know the journey is real because it is imperfect, and it is imperfect because it is real. Trust the process, and don't let perfection stifle your progress.

Seeking the important is a vital step in setting your energy clock for success. Now, let's set your energy clock for success.

SETTING YOUR ENERGY CLOCK

IT'S ONE THING TO KNOW THAT MANAGING OUR ENERGY is important, and it is another to be intentional about doing it personally and professionally. It is another to make it real. To make it happen. To make it a part of our daily lives with our culture at work, our teams, our families. If we set our energy clock with intention, we will live a life of purpose. If we simply let the day run as it will, it is far too easy to be swept up in energy draining activities hour by hour and day after day.

EMBRACE CHANGE

"The secret of change is to focus all of your energy, not on fighting the old, but on building the new."
—DAN MILLMAN, AUTHOR

HOW DO THE BEST MAINTAIN A HIGH LEVEL OF SUCCESS? I asked Geno Auriemma, University of Connecticut's legendary basketball coach, and he told me something I didn't expect. He said he is always seeking ways to improve. To change. And that the best time to change is when things are going well.

This is a guy who (at time of publication) has won more than one thousand games and eleven national championships! Wouldn't that record of consistency tell you he was good at putting his energy toward the same things over and over?

Yes and no. The winning was consistent. However, behind the scenes, he never stopped learning and adapting. He was always embracing ways to pivot (pun intended).

Those who sustain success make it a point to listen. They take it on themselves to call people in and outside of their industries who they can learn from. They always want to evolve for the better.

Kobe Bryant is another star known for embracing change, for asking for feedback from others in all spaces. Here's a small list of people he's cold-called.

+ Nike CEO Mark Parker
+ Apple Chief Design Officer Jony Ive
+ Oprah Winfrey
+ Media mogul Arianna Huffington
+ Actress Hilary Swank

So it should come as no surprise that Bryant's post-basketball accolades include an Oscar for his animated-short film and a two-hundred-million-dollar windfall from a six-million-dollar investment in sports drink BodyArmor.

The best stay curious about how to employ their energy for the greatest results.

Because here is the deal: Don't wait until the bottom falls out to change. This is a major thing I have seen with the best athletes and coaches: *They lean into it before they have to.*

Coaches don't start asking for advice from others when they are a few losses away from getting fired, and the best leaders don't ask for advice after they or their teams have missed quota month over month.

They are always ahead of that. Why? Because they recognize change is constant, and to stay relevant, it's best to lead change than to fight change.

As we ask, as we listen, we might just pivot a smidge with something that we learn that we can tweak and try. Or maybe that information gives you a sharper eye. Now something is showing up for you or your team that appears to be draining, or inefficient, or worst of all, unsustainable.

We can all think of organizations that fought the needed change and are now out of business. Blockbuster, Kodak, and PanAm come to mind. We can spend time fighting the change or we can open our minds and hearts and look through the fuzzy glass and ask ourselves, *What will it look like if we lean into it? What might be on the other side of that uncertainty if we try? What's at risk to take a chance*?

It takes energy to change, yes. But it also takes energy to resist. To stay in place. The best know there are better places to expend their energy than in spinning their wheels.

And you know what? Maybe, just maybe, that change will make it more fun.

CREATE SYSTEMS

"Make systems conscious,
creative, and joyful."

—CHRIS BARÉZ-BROWN, AUTHOR AND ENTREPRENEUR

EVERY DAY, LOOK AT SOMETHING YOU DO THAT YOU'VE always done and ask yourself, *Why?*

Great leaders know that great systems maximize energy while staying creative and innovative along the way. Great systems are actually great habits. A system doesn't just solve a problem. It keeps a good habit going. The problem is sometimes it keeps a bad habit going too.

If systems are simply automating our habits, we can use systems to aid our success by staying aware of how we are using them and what patterns form, but if we simply use systems to automate *everything*, including ourselves, we will fall back into the trap of simply

moving forward, staying busy, and equate being busy with accomplishing.

So how can you both automate *and* stay engaged? Let's look at problem-solving first. Have you ever solved a similar problem more than once? The second time you solve it is more frustrating than the first, right?

If the problem is something that could easily show up again, you'll want to be sure to create a system instead of place a Band-Aid on the issue. Put steps in place so that problem is handled well the next time, based on how you solved it the last time. Create the wheel, and let it turn. Don't recreate the wheel. That's a waste of energy!

What about habits that are working for you? What systems keep those going? How do you invest some energy to keep those turning?

But—here is the big *but*—I like what my friend and innovation guru Chris Baréz-Brown says about systems: "Make systems conscious, creative, and joyful." In other words, systematize with intention and be wary of autopilot, because otherwise we aren't really present.

Great systems adapt to change by using minimal energy. Create systems that work for you, so you can put your energy into what matters most.

EMBRACE THE PROCESS

"A good process produces good results."

—NICK SABAN, FOOTBALL COACH

THIS IS WHERE IT GETS REAL WITH THE CLARITY YOU have created through your energy audit. Now it's time to live in a way that is aligned with that clarity. It's about being intentional and disciplined. We have to take that awareness and turn it into action.

Let's start by looking at your calendar and going one step further with your energy audit. I do this by literally looking at one week at a time and color-coding what's existing on my calendar—meetings, travel, family commitments, appointments. I then assign it a color—green (*energizer!*), orange (*blah*), or red (*ugh!*). See the next page for just the first three days in my planner as an example of how to plan your week according to your energy clock:

MY PLANNER

	MONDAY	TUESDAY	WEDNESDAY
6am	Prayer	Prayer	Prayer
7am	Yoga	Weights	Workout
	Email Cleanup	Email Cleanup	Email Cleanup
8am		Parent-Teacher Conference	A/V Check
			Meet & Greet
9am	Team Check-In Call	Coffee With SK	Keynote in Vegas
10am		Podcast Interview	Book Signing
	Keynote Prep Call #1		
11am	Keynote Prep Call #2		Car to Airport (Client Call)
12pm	Lunch with Fred	Board Meeting	Flight to Atlanta
1pm	Game-changer Prep Call		
2pm	10 Best Practices of Negotiation Webinar	Call JC	
3pm		Call EL	
4pm	Business Development Weekly Wrap-Up Report	Car to Airport	Volleyball Game at School
5pm	Email Cleanup	Email Cleanup	Email Cleanup
6pm		Flight to Vegas	

Now you can clearly see the week ahead. Just by glancing at the colors, you can see where you are likely to feel your energy dip and where you might need to make some changes.

We'll start with protecting your finite resource: your time. When you protect your time, you are choosing what you give your energy to as well. Think about your energy audit. What are the things that maximize your energy? Wouldn't it be a game-changer if you incorporated one to three of your energy-making, fulfilling activities from your green zone *every day*?

Now let's execute that against reality. Your calendar is a shield for protecting this sacred time so that others can't capture it first. Time to build in our energizers!

With this goal in mind, pick a day of the week—maybe Friday as you close out your week or Sunday nights—to go over your calendar and protect your green zone. I go out about thirty days and block off times for the activities I know give me energy. I make these important by planning ahead and blocking the time on my calendar. If the time isn't blocked, it's easily taken, and maybe by something that *doesn't* give me energy.

It's far easier to protect something that's already on your schedule than to try to cram it in there later.

How far you go out in your calendar is up to you. You might just need to go out to the next week, or you might need to go out a few weeks or even months. In your world, to protect your energy by protecting this time, what works best?

It may not be obvious at first. Let go of perfect and work with it over the next several months. It's different for everyone and every team.

Trust me, you need a way to ensure that your energy booster times are protected. Only you can guarantee that inside of each day are activities or events or simply moments that fill you up and give you energy. Then and only then are you setting yourself up for success.

Leaders, knowing the things that are in the green zone for your teams and being intentional about prioritizing those is imperative to building healthy connections. Knowing the things that are in the red zone is equally important. For example, I have an employee that "hates" when I send her a "list" of things, so I work to avoid doing this as it zaps her energy. Instead, I might get on the phone and talk through it or just send the high-level ask and marry the ask with questions to unlock answers from her, which provides me with the result we both want most. As leaders, learning what tasks and responsibilities your team feels fall in the red zone—then helping them navigate and/or lessen their impact—will help lift your team to their best selves. The byproduct for you—as a leader—is that you will see better results.

This practice takes discipline—but it's ultimately protecting the energy you bring to the people and things that matter most in life.

Pick a time of week and day to set your clock. Set it—and protect it.

ANTICIPATE

"Anticipate the difficult by
managing the easy."
—LAO TZU, CHINESE PHILOSOPHER

A KEY PART OF SETTING YOUR ENERGY CLOCK IS ANTIC-
ipating the red zone. Identify the things that are draining
your energy—the people, situations, and moments that
deplete your energy quicker than normal. Even when
these might be important, you are left with less energy.

You'll always need to pay attention to the energy
drainers. Go back and review the things you wrote in
the red zone of your energy audit. What's there? When
is it showing up on your calendar?

This means that as you set your energy clock to
protect the green zone, you should also take note of
the orange and red zones—the moments, meetings,
and activities that tend to drain you or are just mundane

yet necessary. What can you do after these activities to move yourself back up toward green? What works for you? Maybe a quick walk outside or a conversation with a favorite colleague? What are you bookending those with so you can ensure you can move in and through those moments smoothly without them dominating and completely draining your energy?

It can be as simple as adjusting your calendar to build in mini-breaks so that after back-to-back meetings, you have a thirty-minute window to reflect before moving on to the next thing.

Or after a long business trip out of town, block off the following morning at work so you can get your head on straight before new things start flying at you. Or, if you are a leader, schedule time to connect with your team and give them your presence and energy.

Energy boosters before or after things that take you to the orange and red zones will ensure you have the energy you need for what matters most to you.

Remember, it's all about the energy we bring to our time. It's about rebooting, re-engaging, and preparing to show back up better, fuller, and more eager to connect and serve those that matter most.

I am not suggesting any of this is easy, but I am suggesting it is possible. It might require a conversation with your boss so she knows that when a time slot on your calendar says "green zone," it identifies time you are protecting. She knows you're aware of your energy drains and how to bring your best self to your team's work.

RECOVERY AND RESET

"It's not whether you get knocked down, it's whether you get up."
—VINCE LOMBARDI, FOOTBALL COACH

THROUGHOUT THIS JOURNEY, YOU MIGHT FALL SHORT, get frustrated, and experience days that don't go right—including full days or weeks where you feel like you are only living in the orange and red zone. The key to this issue is to recognize it quickly and be intentional about shifting out of it.

It's important to know how to flow through each zone smoothly, calmly, and with control of your head and heart. Let me share some experiences of moving through these zones, including what I have found works and what doesn't work.

For me, a *green* activity is yoga. Heated power yoga to be more specific. I found a studio with a vibe I love and a community of people I respect and enjoy.

When I go there, I turn off my phone and work to be present. When I walk out and turn my phone on, the emails and texts immediately populate the screen. Right off this Zen state, I come back to the real world—emails, voicemails, good news, or bad news.

Whatever it is I have found that day in my yoga practice, I take it with me as I'm walking out. I sit in my car, taking a moment to absorb it and reflect. As my yoga teacher says, "Take your yoga practice off your mat and into your life."

Just that five or ten minutes helps me flow more in and through the different zones of my energy clock as I take in my texts and emails. As I make decisions about who or what to give my energy to, I have what I need to handle the drainers and the obligations with control and ease.

In all of our work, there are things that decrease our energy but are part of the process toward growth. A perfect example for me is airplanes. They can suck some energy out of you, that is for sure, but one of the things that gives me the most energy is speaking and connecting to an audience—big or small. The moment I walk on stage and they think, "All right, lady, what do you have for me? I am busy," to the laughing, the tears, the head nods, the engagement, the smiles, and the personal connections afterward… Boy, does that fill me up. But I have to do something that doesn't fill me up first in order to flow into something so magically special to me. We all have things like this in our lives, and finding that perfect balance of how much is too much, and how much is just right, is the key.

Here's another example of real-life flow through the green, orange, and reds. The other day, I landed in Atlanta at 3:02 p.m. after two keynotes. One had been in Phoenix and the other in Dallas.

Looking at my watch, I think, *I could make my daughter's volleyball game if I really hustle*. Her match starts at 4:00 p.m. So as I am walking off the plane, I think, *I got this, I can make it in time. Awesome, what fun, but I've got to fly.*

By 3:18 p.m., I am in a car. I feel myself flowing to the red as I press the driver to get in the left lane. By 3:38 p.m., I'm home, but the dogs should go out before I head to the school gym.

I drop my bags, let the dogs out, and bark at them to go "tee-tee and poopy" before I get in my car to get to the school. It's now 3:45 p.m., and the school is fifteen minutes away.

I drive fast, round corners, zipping through yellow lights. I'm hot when I hit traffic or red lights. "*Go,* people!"

At 3:57 p.m., I pull into a parking space, jump out of the car, run inside, and find a spot in the bleachers. My daughter sees me enter the gym, and my heart immediately feels full.

After the game, it's another story.

"Mom, can you take Chloe home, and can Ashley spend the night tonight? And can we stop and get dinner before you drop Chloe off?"

As my daughter and her friends pile into the car,

not really understanding the chain of events through-out the day or my fire drill to get here, I put all that aside. Because if I don't, I'll slip in the red zone, when my whole goal was to shift to green.

"How was your day, angel?" I ask my daughter.

"It was good, Mom! That math test, I think I did pretty well, but listen to this…"

I smile inside that I get to hear this story when it's fresh.

In those few moments, I flowed through the zones, as we so often do, but I stayed aware of it and worked to be intentional to shift to the green when I needed to. I got to see my daughter play in her game and heard the stories from school that day fresh off the press.

Once everyone was in their spots, I paused and smiled. So thankful for that moment, reflecting that only a few hours before I was speaking to over a thousand people in ballroom in Dallas. I got energy from work that was important to me, and with some quick thinking and energy bursts, I was able to make my daughter's game. I was loving being in the green zone, even if I had to briefly move through red and orange to get there!

Now, let me acknowledge the times, things, and behaviors in the red zone in our lives that decrease our energy and aren't fulfilling—and, more importantly, how to move out of those moments. These are the moments that if they go unmanaged can be downright destructive. These could be toxic relationships with coworkers, partners, or overly and unrealistically demanding clients. Managing our energy around these unfulfilling drainers is imperative. It's about eliminating what we can, managing what we can't, and squeezing every ounce of good out of these moments available.

I was in the orange and red most of the day during my very first job in Atlanta. It was with the Super Bowl Host Committee, the central planning hub that managed hundreds of daily requests and inquiries in the year leading up to the big game. I was part of a small team that worked in a big building downtown with no windows, which kind of tells you where this story is going.

The job sounded important, but it sure didn't feel that way. We fielded calls from NFL executives and the chief marketing officers of big brands such as Coca-Cola, Home Depot, and Chick-fil-A. Hundreds of times a day you could hear me say the same six words: "Super Bowl Twenty-Eight, this is Molly." I was the receptionist.

I worked for a supervisor (I'll call her Jane) who came in late, sat in her office, often with the door closed, and talked to her friends—weaving in a few work calls when she felt like it. She enjoyed keeping callers on hold—a power play. Every time Jane told some well-known person to hold the line for no reason other than her own ego, no matter how much I begged, she took her sweet time.

Sometimes the bigwigs would hang up, sometimes they would light me up, sometimes they would want to talk to her boss (who was a nice guy), but the best was when they would come to the office—eventually they all did—and they got to see the circus act in person.

Hell of a first job, right?

In the middle of these ridiculous office games, I worried that I had nowhere to go beyond answering the phones and trying to get dysfunctional Jane to pick up the line. To top it off, this was in the winter—of course—so I would get to the office when it was dark, and I would leave when it was dark. Sounds fun, right? I felt unfulfilled and drained every time I got in my car to head to the office *and* when I left. I was living in the red zone, and I hated it.

There were moments, rare ones but enough of them, to keep me going. When the executives—the corporate sponsors—would come up to the office for meetings, they would be in the front lobby doing nothing else (people didn't have cell phones then—yes, I am old!). That was my moment. When all these bigwigs were waiting, I could talk with them, ask for advice—I had one goal inside these moments, what I wanted most of all was…

…to get them to like and respect me enough to hire me or help me!

When I began to move from these moments of feeling totally unfulfilled and drained to moments of opportunity and connection, I knew I was getting somewhere. It was about shifting my mindset to *what if*. Of course, I didn't know it at the time, but I was practicing moving from red to orange to green and recognizing that my energy was in my control!

The flow in and out of these zones was so real throughout the day. The truth is, it was life-changing. Had I just remained in the red, I would have missed out. By seeing an opportunity in the middle of the unfulfilling, draining work, I connected with these incredible people. They ended up helping to connect me with other incredible people. They sparked progress in my career and comfort with my new city.

These opportunities gave me momentum. I

developed a goal of connecting with every person who called the main line or set foot in our office. It was clear they could make a difference in my career, and one day, I might help them as well. After the Super Bowl, I had a sizable list of VIPs I could turn to for advice, and those contacts led me to my career as a sports agent.

There's never more energy than when moving from that red zone to the green zone. When you take a drainer and make it an energy booster, you have an absolute rocket in your life!

SETTING YOUR ENERGY CLOCK

**"Hold an image of the life you want
and that image will become fact."**

—NORMAN VINCENT PEALE, AUTHOR

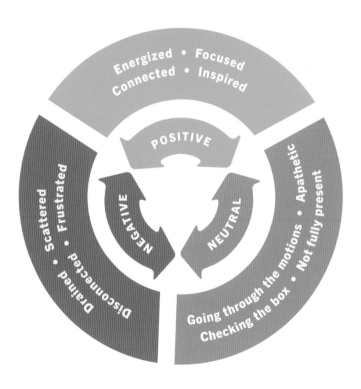

Review an audit for yourself, completing each category below:

MAXIMIZE

What increases your energy and is meaningful to you?

+
+
+
+
+

BE EFFICIENT

What doesn't necessarily increase or decrease your energy but exists?

•
•
•
•
•

ELIMINATE OR MANAGE

What decreases your energy?

–
–
–
–
–

You owe it to yourself and those who matter most to you to set your energy clock. It will take courage—lean in. You will have days that are more difficult than others; recover fast. Setting your energy clock will create a life of clarity, connection, and fulfillment, so start here:

1. Do the energy audit.

2. Color-code your calendar and make adjustments accordingly.

3. Choose an accountability partner, and share your energy audit with them.

4. Hold monthly check-ins with your accountability partner.

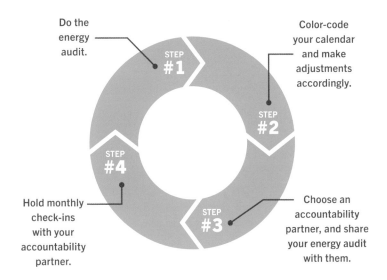

Getting to the end of our lives and looking back with a full heart, feeling like we gave our energy to the things and people that matter most, is *not* an accident. In fact, it is far from it. It requires clarity and intentional thought and behavior.

My deepest desire for you is that *The Energy Clock* helps you live a life that aligns your energy with your time in order to make your greatest impact.

ABOUT THE AUTHOR

MOLLY FLETCHER is a trailblazer in every sense of the word—a rare talent of business wisdom, relationship brilliance, and unwavering optimism. A popular keynote speaker, she shares the unconventional techniques that helped her thrive as one of the first female sports agents in the high-stakes, big-ego world of professional sports and, now, as a successful entrepreneur.

Formerly, as president of client representation for sports and entertainment agency CSE, Fletcher spent two decades as one of the world's only female sports agents. She was hailed as the "female Jerry Maguire" by CNN as she recruited and represented hundreds of sport's biggest names, including Hall of Fame pitcher John Smoltz, PGA Tour golfer Matt Kuchar, broadcaster Erin Andrews, and basketball championship coaches Tom Izzo and Doc Rivers.

As she successfully negotiated over five hundred million dollars in contracts and built lasting relationships, she also observed and adopted the traits of those at the top of their game.

Molly's energy and passion for life shines through everything she does. She finds her greatest joy at home in Atlanta with her husband Fred and their three daughters.

THE
MOLLY
FLETCHER
COMPANY

INSPIRING GAME CHANGERS

**Hailed as the
"Female Jerry Maguire"
by CNN**

www.theenergyclock.com

Game On! with Molly Fletcher

is Molly's weekly newsletter with inspiration to kick off your week. Every Tuesday, Molly will send you something to read, watch, and listen to—plus a few extras—on your journey to unleashing your potential!

▸ *Subscribe at MollyFletcher.com!*

Game Changers with Molly Fletcher

is a podcast designed to help maximize your influence. In each episode, Molly takes you behind the scenes with peak performers to learn what makes them tick and discover how to apply their lessons to your life.

▸ *Subscribe on iTunes!*

Game Changer Negotiation Training

is an exclusive in-house, one-day negotiation workshop for your team. You'll learn our proven approach to successful negotiation so you can ask for what you want, create value for both sides, and close more deals.

▸ *Visit GameChanger360.com!*

LOOK FOR MOLLY'S OTHER BOOKS!

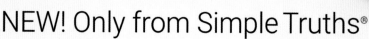

NEW! Only from Simple Truths®

spark impact in just one hour

IGNITE READS IS A NEW SERIES OF 1-HOUR READS WRITTEN BY WORLD-RENOWNED EXPERTS!

These captivating books will help you become the best version of yourself, allowing for new opportunities in your personal and professional life. Accelerate your career and expand your knowledge with these powerful books written on today's hottest ideas.

TRENDING BUSINESS AND PERSONAL GROWTH TOPICS

 Read in an hour or less

 Leading experts and authors

 Bold design and captivating content

EXCLUSIVELY AVAILABLE ON SIMPLETRUTHS.COM

Need a training framework?
Engage your team with discussion guides and PowerPoints for training events or meetings.

Want your own branded editions?
Express gratitude, appreciation, and instill positive perceptions to staff or clients by adding your organization's logo to your edition of the book.

Add a supplemental visual experience
to any meeting, training, or event.

Contact us for special corporate discounts!
(800) 900-3427 x247 or simpletruths@sourcebooks.com

LOVED WHAT YOU READ AND WANT MORE?

Sign up today and be the FIRST to receive advance copies of Simple Truths® NEW releases written and signed by expert authors. Enjoy a complete package of supplemental materials that can help you host or lead a successful event. This high-value program will uplift you to be the best version of yourself!

— SIMPLE TRUTHS —

ELITE CLUB

ONE MONTH. ONE BOOK. ONE HOUR.

Your monthly dose of motivation, inspiration, and personal growth.